Nancy Ross and Sara Hanks: Where Must We Stand?

(Note this conversation was recorded on July 27, 2018 in Sandy, Utah. I will use GT for Gospel Tangents to indicate when I am talking to them. The interview has been lightly edited to remove verbal miscues.)

Introduction

Welcome to Gospel Tangents, the best source for Mormon History, science and theology. I'm Rick Bennett. I'm excited to introduce Sara Hanks and Dr. Nancy Ross from Dixie State University. I'll let them introduce themselves more in a minute, but we're going to talk about their latest book, "Where We Must Stand." It's about 10 years of the Feminist Mormon Housewives blog, so we'll get to know them a little bit better. Check out our conversation.

Contents

Feminist Successes & Setbacks

Introduction

Dr. Nancy Ross and Sara Hanks, co-authors of "Where We Must Stand" discuss their experiences blogging at _Feminist Mormon Housewives_,[1] and putting together a book on the first 10 years of the blog. They also discuss successes in pushing for change within the LDS Church, and their reactions to Kate Kelly's excommunication. Check out our conversation...

The Interview

GT: 00:00:46 Well, welcome to Gospel tangents podcast. I'd like to have you guys both introduce yourself. Let's start with you.

Nancy: 00:00:51 So I'm Nancy Ross and I am a professor at a university in southern Utah.

GT: 00:00:58 You can tell us the university.

Nancy: 00:00:59 Dixie State University. And I'm an art historian by training. So, I have a Ph.D. in art history. But about a year ago I changed departments into an interdisciplinary studies department, because a lot of what I do these days with research and projects doesn't really focus around art history. It's actually focuses more in Mormon Studies and so yeah, I'm a medieval art historian who moonlight as a sociologist of religion and I do a lot of Mormon Studies stuff. So that's kind of what I do.

---

[1] See https://www.feministmormonhousewives.org/

GT: 00:01:32   That's fantastic. And tell us about yourself.

Sara: 00:01:35   Yeah. My name is Sara Hanks. I'm a mom of two, a stay at home mom, freelance writer, part time editorial assistant. I was born and raised in Utah and still live [here.] I live in Layton at this point and I am a former blogger at Feminist Mormon Housewives (FMH) blog, which is how I got involved making this book about Feminist Mormon Housewives.

GT: 00:02:02   Why don't you show us your book?

Sara: 00:02:02   This is the book!

GT: 00:02:02   "Where We Must Stand."[2]

Sara: 00:02:06   Yes, "Where We Must Stand: 10 years of Feminist Mormon Housewives."

GT: 00:02:12   So that's actually why we brought you in. You guys are both co-authors. Tell us a little bit about the book. What got you involved with that?

Sara: 00:02:22   Yeah, so I began blogging. Feminist Mormon Housewives is a blog that's been around since 2004. It's a group blog, focusing on women's issues in the Mormon church, women's experiences and stories. And that blog began in 2004. I read it for a very long time and in 2013 I was invited to come on as one of the bloggers and one year later in 2014 was the 10th anniversary and it just seemed very momentous, like the blog has been around for 10 years. It's produced so

---

much content. They are such a thriving community. It's been a very interesting 10 years, like there's been a complete story. And so, I just liked the idea of making a book about it and talked to my other bloggers and they said, well, if you want to do that, we support you. I didn't know how to do it, but I figured I could figure it out. And so that was the starting point and that was four years ago. So, it took a long time to actually come to fruition. But that was my interest in it as a member of the community for a long time and one of the bloggers.

GT: 00:03:31 So, how did you decide what to include? Because you didn't include every blog post.

Sara: 00:03:31 No, there were over 4,000 blog posts published in those 10 years. It could fill an entire bookshelf if that was all in book form. So, I mean it was a really painstaking process. The first part was just to read all of them. And any of them that stood out to me as particularly whatever--particularly interesting or relevant or funny or well written or whatever, I would just sort of make a note. I had this running list of blog posts that I thought might be good contenders. And by the end of that, I mean I had hundreds of options. And so, then we had to narrow it down and narrow it down. I had what I thought was going to be kind of like a final list and we were looking to publish the book in two volumes. And so, there was room for a lot more, but then decided that we needed to have it in one volume and that was when Nancy came on board about a year ago. And so, she really helped look at that list that I thought we couldn't take anything away from and we had to cut it down by I think more than half.

GT: 00:04:33   Oh really?

Nancy: 00:04:33   Yeah. I think when I first started there were about 300,000 words of text and I think the book ended up at about 140,000 words of text. And so, because it's like a paperback, right? The binding can only take so much stress.

Sara: 00:04:49   Right.

Nancy: 00:04:49   So we figured we could have a really big book but we couldn't have like a super-size book. So, what we did...

GT: 00:04:57   Not a Michael Quinn book.

Both: 00:04:58   Not a Michael Quinn Book.

Nancy: 00:04:59   No, love him, love his work.

Sara: 00:05:01   Oh obviously.

Nancy: 00:05:01   But, you need a hard back for that. And we were trying to self-publish.

Sara: 00:05:07   So I mean then we just took that list down by a lot. I think the final count of blog posts in the book is 136. And we tried to develop themes. We tried to say, okay, how did the community deal with this particular issue over time? We had to make some tough calls as far as, here are lots of good posts on a certain subject, but these ones are shorter, so we have to choose these. And I mean there were dozens of factors that went into deciding each theme. We wanted to make sure that different writers were represented appropriately. If somebody contributed a lot of content to the blog over the years, we wanted to make sure that that was reflected as well. And anyway.

Nancy: 00:05:56   So ultimately after a couple of rounds or after I read everything that Sara had, we decided that we were going to refine it down to a couple of really key themes that were really central to the blog over its first decade. And Motherhood was one of those biggest of themes. It really started. Lisa Patterson Butterworth founded the blog and part of that was out of the loneliness of being a young mother at home with young children. And so, the theme of motherhood and then the different ways in which people experienced Motherhood: Motherhood with disability. Trying to become a mother but experiencing infertility.

Sara: 00:06:34   Not wanting to be a mother, as a Mormon woman, you know, that's a very strained place to be.

Nancy: 00:06:42   Yeah. And so, we've got a lot of like motherhood and motherhood themed posts. There are a number of posts that referenced Heavenly Mother. There are posts that reference modesty, like sexuality and modesty, it's as a big and important theme that kind of runs throughout the book. Activism is an important theme that runs throughout the book. And so, we tried to be [ask] well, what do we see as these big themes from our experience? And then how do we make the book flow because all the posts will be connected to some common themes and threads.

GT: 00:07:19   I did notice that. I'm trying to remember what year it was when Kate Kelly got excommunicated.

Nancy: 00:07:25   2014.

GT: 00:07:25   2014, That was a big theme for that entire year it seems like.

Sara: 00:07:28   Yeah, it was. Yeah, it dominated the landscape for sure.

Nancy: 00:07:33   But at that time the community was all about activism, or so much of the community conversation turned to activism. Really. In the middle of 2012, and this is covered in the book, there's a little activist action to try and better understand different temples' policies with regard to women and young women doing baptisms for the dead while menstruating. And so, there are a bunch of phone calls made and they try to get information about what different temples policies are with the idea that, you might show up at a temple and they might have a different policy and that might make people feel excluded or embarrassed.

Sara: 00:08:13   Embarrassed. Yeah.

Nancy: 00:08:14   And so that happens in the middle of 2012. By the end of 2012, we've got the first "Wear pants to church day," and then that's followed by, "Let

Women Pray," and the advent of "Let Women Pray" was its own activist event to try and ask church leaders to let a woman pray in general conference which happened with Jean Stephens, which is super exciting.

Sara: 00:08:35   Yeah.

Nancy: 00:08:36   And then we've got the arrival of Ordain Women in the Spring of 2013. And so, leading up to Kate Kelly's excommunication, like from the middle of 2012 to the middle of 2014, there was just so much momentum in the community for like, Hey, we can change things. With the temple baptisms issue, after all of this information gathering, someone was able to kind of make a connection further up the chain in the church and then the church issued a clarification to say no, we need all the temples to allow women and young women to participate in baptisms regardless of whether or not they're menstruating. And that was, that felt huge.

Sara: 00:09:15   Oh yeah. Because this whole time, I mean that was like eight years into FMH's existence and sort of the rebuilding of the Mormon feminist community. And all that time it had felt like we were having these very important conversations, but just with each other. We were like, "I wonder if they even know we exist?" Like if the church as an organization or you know, leaders or the bureaucracy. And so that moment with the temple issue, it did really feel like, "Whoa. Like we could have some impact even in these smaller areas. You know, what if we allowed ourselves to imagine that possibility instead of just thinking that this had to be a private matter? What if we could be activists basically?"

Nancy: 00:10:03   And, even just little tiny moments of acknowledgement, just built up so much hope for change in the community. And I remember feeling such intense hope for change. It's like, wow, this is such an exciting time to be a Mormon woman because we are asking for things and those requests are being acknowledged and sometimes granted, and so when it was announced in advance of conference that Jean Stevens was going to pray, it felt like a huge moment of triumph.

Sara: 00:10:33   Absolutely.

Sara: 00:10:34   And it's difficult to [remember back.] Like everything that's happened in the last few years, it's difficult to revisit and kind of embody that moment of triumph because we all know that like that, that wasn't going to last, right? Like things weren't going to play out in the way that we hoped.

GT: 00:10:49   That was the high water mark.

Nancy: 00:10:49   Right! But it was, it just felt, it felt so good. It felt so hopeful. Personally, I felt very secure. Like when Kate Kelly was excommunicated, I was a Relief Society teacher and I just felt--not quite at that tense moment, but in the run up to a lot of that I just felt like this is a great moment to be a Mormon woman and I feel so hopeful that I can ask a question and that the church will hear me and that they will respond positively and try to make space for more people like me. And that just felt like a truly wonderful, hopeful thing, where that wasn't really the feeling I had had prior to that point. And so, I mean there was just that momentum for hope just really consumed the community and it was a beautiful thing. Like, I know it wasn't going to last and, and things weren't going to end the way we wanted them to, but those were truly great moments for the community to come together, to be like, "We can affect change," and that was just a really great thing.

Sara: 00:11:55   Yeah.

GT: 00:11:56   Great. So, tell us what [happened] with Kate Kelly, because that's really where the book kind of ends, it seems like.

Sara: 00:12:02   Yeah. It's completely by coincidence. That was the 10-year mark.

Nancy: 00:12:05   Yeah.

GT: 00:12:06   And so, so you have this high watermark where women can pray in conference and you have the temple baptism issue that it was taken care of, and then talk about the feelings when Kate Kelly was excommunicated.

Nancy: 00:12:22   Oh.

Sara: 00:12:25 I mean, I think one part of it, one part of the feeling was just so much shock, because not only had we felt really hopeful for the possibilities of change, but we also kind of were under the impression as a community at large that with the advent of the Internet and so much attention being paid to the church and so much possibility for exposing problems or injustices that the church wouldn't take the sort of actions that they had taken when it came to Sonia Johnson in the 70's or the September Six in the early 90's or the professors at BYU who were censured. We thought, "They wouldn't because it would be too much of a risk. There would be too much backlash."

Nancy: 00:13:17 And it was also right in the middle of that Mormon moment. And the church had done the "I'm a Mormon" campaign. They had spent so much time, effort, energy and resources trying to make the church look good in the eyes of the public.

Sara: 00:13:28 Right.

Nancy: 00:13:29 So with the Romney campaign, there was so much effort to try and revamp the Church as modern and more inclusive than people maybe had had guessed.

Sara: 00:13:39 And there's room for everyone and there were conference talks to that effect, you know, as far as there is room for you here I think is what, Elder Uchtdorf said. And, we felt like there was [room for us.] I don't think there were very many supporters of Ordain Women or Mormon feminists who were expecting an announcement about women's ordination, like any second, you know? That wasn't the expectation. But for a year Ordain Women had existed. Kate Kelly talks in the book, actually there's a guest post from her where she talks about meeting with her bishop and how he wanted to make sure that she knew there was no danger of any disciplinary action, and that she was welcomed. And there was this feeling that "Okay, we're not going to get what we're asking for, but it's okay that we're asking." That's not a problem.

Sara: <u>00:14:30</u>   And so yeah, it just really came as a shock. I mean, so I think that was one element of the feeling at that time. Just really quickly, there's a post in the book that I think of a lot from Joanna Brooks. And it was right after the announcement that both Kate Kelly and John Dehlin were going to be facing disciplinary action. That announcement came. The announcement of both of those people facing discipline came on the same day and so we were really grappling with it as a community and Joanna writes about [it.] The name of her post is "let it be different this time."[3] Even after knowing that these courts are going to happen, there was still a little piece of our hearts that was like, well maybe it'll be okay, like maybe some higher up will swoop in and fix it. So just we were just shocked, I think.

---

[3] See https://www.feministmormonhousewives.org/2014/06/let-it-be-different-this-time/

Nancy: <u>00:15:18</u>

That was definitely my feeling. I had felt, and I think a lot of us felt that the Church was a much more moderate institution and especially with things like the "I'm a Mormon" campaign, that it was trying to be a little more mainstream and a little less exclusive. Right? And, it was a little less concerned with things like boundary maintenance. And of course, we were wrong. We were wrong. It was. The Church was still very concerned with boundary maintenance and it wasn't the more moderate institution that we felt it had become. And so, I was on that first board of Ordain Women[4] and I was in the room when Kate Kelly got the information from her bishop that she had been excommunicated and it was devastating. And up into like literally up until that moment, I had had this very firm belief, as Sara just said that somebody was going to intervene and realize the harm that would be done to the church through this thing and that they would put a stop to it or put a stop to the idea that you can't still claim that it's okay for women to ask questions about women's issues and excommunicate Kate Kelly.

Nancy: <u>00:16:29</u>

Like, you can't claim on the one hand that that's okay, and then be excommunicating people for doing that exact same thing on the other hand. And that somebody would put a stop to the nonsense. But ultimately what I discovered is that nobody was going to put a stop to that nonsense. And, she was excommunicated and that was such a shock to my system. I know that other people in

---

[4] See https://ordainwomen.org/

that room and on that board at that time had a much greater sense of what was going to happen. The church really hadn't changed and that this was the most likely outcome. But, for me and a few other people in that room that was not. We had so much hope and had so much tremendous hope that really made us naive to particular realities of the church.

Sara: 00:17:15   Right.

Nancy: 00:17:15   And to say that it was devastating isn't quite strong enough a term.

Sara: 00:17:21   It really, I feel like for many people, it shifted their entire posture towards the church and towards being a woman and a feminist in a patriarchal institution. And so, another thing about it is that it wasn't simply about Kate as a person, it was also about Kate as a symbol, as a representative of the community. But it was also about the fact that dozens of other people who didn't have name recognition that Kate had, were experiencing discipline of their own. You know, there were some bishops and stake presidents who felt emboldened by the high-profile nature of Kate's discipline to kind of clamp down on people in their own wards. And so, in these Mormon feminist groups and communities, there was a lot of, "Oh, did you hear about so and so? She had her temple recommend taken away." Or this person. And so, it kind of felt like an onslaught of things happening and more and more disillusionment.

Sara & Nancy's Spiritual Journey

Introduction

After the disappointment with Kate Kelly's excommunication, how did Nancy and Sara react? Are they still active in the LDS Church? Check out their answers!

GT: 00:18:21 I know, Nancy, I've followed you a little bit more. I know you're no longer a member of the LDS Church. Was this kind of the first straw that broke the camel's back?

Nancy: 00:18:33 So for me personally, I was in the room when Kate Kelly found out that she was excommunicated and then had to go back to church the next Sunday and teach Relief Society in my very conservative southern Utah ward. And that was a very tense moment and that hope piece of my faith, I would say that that hope piece broke. Ultimately in the coming months after that I was able to rehabilitate my sense of hope, but that happened in a different way. But for me, the end of my participation in the LDS Church really came with the exclusion policy and the leaking of the Exclusion policy in November 2015.[5] And then it was after that I realized that I really couldn't. I really couldn't be part of the LDS Church anymore. And that was an extremely painful, painful thing, right?

---

[5] See https://www.washingtonpost.com/news/acts-of-faith/wp/2015/11/05/mormon-church-to-exclude-children-of-same-sex-couples-from-getting-blessed-and-baptized-until-they-are-18/?noredirect=on&utm_term=.ab658f71b1b2

Nancy: <u>00:19:31</u>   Like I had the strength to kind of pick myself up and go back and teach Relief Society and face a lot of women who had a lot of anger and disappointment with me in the face and teach and stand in that room in front of them and teach the Relief Society lesson which took no small amount of courage on my part to kind of keep trying to claim my space in my ward and do that. And that became increasingly difficult. That became extremely difficult after Kate Kelly was excommunicated. But that was something that I was really committed to doing. By the time that I was able to kind of rehabilitate my faith. I was able to find new avenues for me where I could feel hopeful, but by the end of the following year and after the announcement of the exclusion policy, I just felt like I couldn't do this anymore.

Nancy: <u>00:20:22</u>   And I think one thing that people don't understand is that a lot of us, it took a lot of faith to keep going to church, and a lot of commitment to keep going to church after Kate Kelly was excommunicated and a lot of Mormon feminists did stop going to church at that time. But a number stayed and that was a great act of faith. And I think people often look at Mormon feminists and think, "Oh well those people don't have faith," or you know.

GT: <u>00:20:53</u>   They've got one foot out the door.

Nancy: <u>00:20:53</u>   "They've got one foot out the door." Or whatever. And it's like, you know, I am still very much a person of faith. Even if my faith looks different from what it did that time, but Mormon feminists are people of faith. Sure, there are Mormon feminist who identify as atheist and that's fine, but the intense desire that the community had and what we tried to foster or what FMH tried to foster was like, here's how we can do this and make it work. Okay.

Sara: 00:21:20   Right. Like that was the whole point.

Nancy: 00:21:21   That was the whole point. And, I think that that's an expression of faith.

Sara: 00:21:26   Right.

Nancy: 00:21:28   And, that is a piece that gets lost. And the whole kind of Mormon feminist project is like, okay, how do I reconcile my values, my values of equality and my values that say people need to be treated fairly and appropriately and that people should have all people, should have similar kinds of opportunities? And how do I square that with my church? Right? But I want to make that work. And so, this community is kind of geared around helping people make that work, at least at that time. The FMH community, the Mormon feminist community was like, "How do we help people reconcile these things and navigate the difficulties of those tensions, which is very much an expression of faith, which is a project of faith, which is a project of supporting other people's faith?

Nancy: 00:22:13   And I think that that is something that really gets lost is this whole issue of faith. And yes, you know, people go through faith transitions and one thing that can happen is that people lose faith. But that itself is its own process of faith. That is a process of faith. That has value and this community has done a lot to help women navigate Mormonism and that it's important to keep pointing out that navigating Mormonism as a woman is actually a really difficult thing.

Sara: 00:22:51   Yeah, it is. It is more difficult for some than for others, but there are some things about Mormonism that can present really unique challenges to women. And so, it's okay for people to feel like they need a little assistance in figuring out, "Okay, how do I do this? How do I make this all work together?"

GT: 00:23:15   So, you're still affiliated with Mormonism but not the LDS Church.

Nancy: 00:23:20   Yes, about 18 months ago I was confirmed in Community of Christ and I was one of the people that helped to create the group, the little congregation and that I belong to in St George and I've been doing that ever since and I'm very happy with that. In many ways my Mormon feminist experience has really prepared me to kind of claim a faith for myself that it wasn't necessarily tightly defined by an institution.

Sara: 00:23:49   Yeah.

Nancy: 00:23:49   And I can't really overstate the importance of my Mormon feminism and the development of my faith and in FMH and the development of my faith because I saw a lot of women wrestling with faith and trying to figure it out. And that gave me the courage to really try and figure it out, including leaving and including finding something else that I could feel was healthier for me. And, then pursuing that and in many ways in Community of Christ, I don't feel the same tension between my values and my activism and my religious life that I felt when I was LDS. And so that's a very happy thing for me because I feel like more pieces of my life are in alignment.

GT: 00:24:34   I've interviewed John Hamer,[6] but I still don't feel like I know enough about the Community of Christ. Do they still have Relief Society?

Nancy: 00:24:45   No.

GT: 00:24:45   There's no Relief Society in the Community of Christ. And I do know they allow ordination of women.

Nancy: 00:24:49   Yep.

GT: 00:24:49   Have you been ordained?

Nancy: 00:24:49   I will be on Sunday.

GT: 00:24:50   On Sunday! You are going to be ordained to?

Nancy: 00:24:52   The office of elder.

GT: 00:24:53   Elder. Nice. Okay. So, compare that to the LDS Church. Does that make you excited or...?

---

[6] See https://gospeltangents.com/2018/01/04/a-seventy-apostle-discuss-myths-kirtland-temple/

Nancy: <u>00:25:01</u>   Yeah, I feel very excited about that. There's part of my Mormon baggage that I can't quite get rid of that's also quite nervous and has mixed feelings about that I think. But I am excited about that. In many ways my Mormon feminist community, my FMH community prepared me that my faith journey would be an individual thing. And our faith journeys take us in lots of different places. The LDS Church is very belief statement oriented, right? In the temple recommend interview: "Do you believe that Joseph Smith is a prophet? Do you believe that the current prophet is a prophet?" And that sort of thing. Community of Christ is more values oriented. So, there are shared core values and, often people think that Community of Christ is just like the LDS Church but liberal and that's not really true. Community of Christ isn't.

GT: <u>00:25:55</u>   John Hamer has said that.

Nancy: <u>00:25:57</u>   Yeah.

Sara: <u>00:25:59</u>   John Hamer.

Nancy: <u>00:25:59</u>   We love John, but that's not how I see it. I see it as it's more organized around shared core values and finding ways to live into those shared core values with a restoration heritage. And yes, it's messy and it's very much a work in progress and it's a church that really embraces its sense of continuing revelation. And so, it feels like there is a lot of change in the church and that happens much more rapidly than perhaps in the LDS Church. But ultimately, I see that as a good and exciting thing and I want to be part of that dynamic--figuring out what God is doing in the world today, kind of business and that's good for me. But I can't really overstate the way in which my Mormon feminism helped me get to that place and then I was able to investigate Community of Christ. Then it was like, okay, here's where I am. Here's where I was kind of brought to with Mormon feminism and now Community of Christ can mentor me in that spiritual direction. And for me that's been a very positive thing in my life.

GT: 00:27:13   Well great. You did mention, and I'm going to get to you in just one second, so I don't want you to think I'm leaving you out.

Sara: 00:27:19   Nancy is a very interesting person.

GT: 00:27:20   One question I have is: one of the things you said earlier in the interview was this issue about menstruating women in temple baptisms. So, I know the temple was a big part of your Mormon heritage.

Nancy: 00:27:31   Yes.

GT: 00:27:32   It's very different in the Community of Christ.[7]

Nancy: 00:27:34   It's very different. They don't do temple like LDS people do temples. So, there's the Kirtland Temple. The Community of Christ owns the Kirtland Temple, like a historical restoration

---

[7] See our interview at https://gospeltangents.com/2018/01/07/comparing-lds-rlds-temple-worship/

tradition temple, and also the temple in Independence which is dedicated to peace. And there are no temple recommends and more sacred or secretive practices. Those are public spaces and public spaces for education and for community and worship. And so, it's not the kind of LDS concept of temple.

GT: 00:28:08   Do you miss that temple experience? Because it sounds like it was a pretty important part of your life.

Nancy: 00:28:13   It was. But I think, as I kind of move further in my LDS journey, and started to see the way, and maybe understood more of LDS history and the way in which temple ceremonies and endowments were connected with polygamy, and I have very strong negative feelings about the idea of practicing polygamy for me or practicing polygamy in the eternities. And I see those for me as very negative things and not everyone does and that's fine. But for me, those are not at all attractive and so the more that I understood that the temple in one way could be read as creating and extending polygamy, even if that's not how it's read exactly today within the LDS tradition, was really not something that I want to be a part of. There are also a number of bits in the temple that had been difficult for me.

Nancy: 00:28:59   I had a very positive initial experience with the initiatory and felt that that was a wonderful thing when I first went through. But the endowment did trouble me from the first time I went through. I didn't feel like I could communicate any of that

24

to anyone. And it took a long time before I was able to kind of say aloud, you know, this has always made me feel uncomfortable. The idea that I would covenant to obey my husband. Like nobody ever warned me about the covenant before I went through and that was a really big deal. But nobody had said, "This is what's going to happen. And this is what you're going to need to promise." Because even in my most faithful, loyal LDS believing state that was still going to not be something I wanted to covenant to.

GT: 00:29:45   It sounds like you don't miss that part.

Nancy: 00:29:49   I don't miss that part at all. Like I don't miss that part at all. That part was at one time very special and very important to me even with doubts and reservations. But as time went on, the temple just became more problematic and more complicated. So, I don't miss. I don't miss that at all. And, that's not something that I long for at all.

GT: 00:30:15   Well Sara, it's your turn.

Sara: 00:30:17   Okay.

GT: 00:30:18   We probably should be talking more about the book, but I'm curious about what has been your relationship? Let's go back to the Kate Kelly excommunication because that's kind of the end of the book. Can you talk about your journey since then?

Sara: 00:30:28   Sure. Yeah. So, when Kate was excommunicated, it was only a few months after the second

Priesthood Session action where women requested entrance to the Priesthood Session of General Conference. And I actually lived really close, just a few blocks from the Salt Lake Temple at the time, and I unexpectedly felt called to join them in that action. That was not like me. Like I shy away from controversial stuff by instinct. But I felt compelled to join them. And so, I went, and I had that experience and I felt prompted by the spirit to do that. And all along the way with my Mormon feminism, I felt periodic confirmations from the spirit that even though this was sort of an uncomfortable place to be or uncomfortable questions to ask, that it was fitting.

Sara: 00:31:31   And so when Kate was excommunicated, I felt again surprised. I felt very personally hurt and I had this confluence. I've never been somebody who has very vivid dreams, except for certain times in my life and this was one of those times when I was just having so many dreams centered around attacks on my voice. Like I don't know if this will make sense, but garden sheers at my throat or being choked. And I realized and worked with my therapist at the time to really realize that the thing that I felt most personally was that I believed a lot of the same things that Kate Kelly believed and she had been loud about it and I had been quiet about it, which was the only reason that I wasn't facing the same sort of consequences she was.

Sara: 00:32:23   But also at the same time there was no way of knowing how loud was too loud. It's all up to bishops and stake presidents and individual wards and dynamics. And there's no knowing when you're going to cross a line that somebody says is too far. And so, I felt very scared and I felt I was having panic attacks whenever I would go to church. And so, I felt like I had to kind of take a step back and I didn't go for a few months. I had intended to not go for longer. I was like, I need to take a break of a year. And, I'm such a Mormon girl. I'm such a religiously inclined person that I couldn't even hold to my own expectations. I went back to church after just a few months and started attending again. And I had a very supportive ward at the time.

Sara: 00:33:08   And I loved relating to the people there. But my journey since then has been, it's just gotten more and more nuanced. And I've had to find a way to relate to the church and relate to my own Mormonism that was very different than how I expected it to be growing up. I fully expected to live the most cookie cutter Mormon woman life you could imagine. I thought that that was what I would do. And I was excited to do it. But at a certain point after my own relationship with God and my own understanding of morality and goodness and personal values, after all that shifted, I just got to a point where I thought, "I don't know how well I fit here anymore and I don't know how well this supports me."

Sara: 00:33:58   I don't know how well the church supports me in what I need to do and I don't know how much I can really contribute to the church. Being that I don't share a worldview that most of the people I'm worshiping with seem to hold. And so, it just got complicated and I don't have any way to kind of tie it up with a bow and say, "And then I decided to join a different church." You know, I haven't done the same thing that Nancy [did.]

GT: 00:34:22   You have not joined another church.

Sara: 00:34:23   I haven't joined another church. I'm still Mormon.

GT: 00:34:26   You're still active?

Sara: 00:34:26   I'm not still active. I mean I'm not entirely gone. I still go sometimes. I have two little kids who also goes sometimes. And so, it's an in between phase for sure. I don't know where it'll end up, but I felt like it was a little over a year ago that I had a very clear impression in a Relief Society class that like the 10 years that I had spent clinging to the cliff face, trying to make it work, that I was okay to let go and that I didn't need to keep trying so hard to make it work anymore. That I could just be with God and entertain the possibility that God would be with me wherever I was.

The F-Word: Feminism

Introduction

Lisa Butterworth wrote a post titled the F-Word: Feminism. Is feminism dangerous? Many faithful Latter-day Saints may be concerned that Mormon feminism is a road to apostasy. Is that true? Would the church split like the Community of Christ did over women's ordination? Sara Hanks and Nancy Ross will answer those questions. Check out our conversation....

GT:	00:35:21	So let me ask you a question, both of you. Whoever wants to jump in is fine. I'm trying to figure out my audience. I think most of my audience is still active LDS, although I know I have some non-LDS people, either former Mormons or even never Mormons. But I know, for those who are active, I remember it was in the first chapter. One of my favorite essays was I think Lisa's, where she talked about the f-word: feminism.[8]
Both:	00:35:49	Yes.
GT:	00:35:49	And so I know that there are going to be some people that are going to say, "Well look. She's [Nancy] left the church. She's [Sara] not going to church anymore. Feminism is awful. It's an f-word."
Sara:	00:36:08	It's really dangerous, yeah.

---

[8] See https://www.feministmormonhousewives.org/2006/12/the-f-word-defining-feminism/

GT: 00:36:08   Do you have any ways to assuage that fear for people who are active LDS that are thinking, "I don't know if I should listen to these two people. One is out of the church in one is barely hanging on."

Sara: 00:36:21   Yeah, right.

Nancy: 00:36:21   So one thing I've done is I've surveyed Mormon feminists[9] and when I surveyed Mormon feminists, when we were experiencing that great big bubble of hope during 2012-2014. Yeah. That great big level of hope. I surveyed Mormon feminists in 2013, about 1800 Mormon feminists, and I think it was 70 something percent of that group was active. And most Mormon feminists at that time were active and it was a very exciting time to be active, you know? And, they were active and, overwhelmingly, not only were they active, but they had some kind of calling. And many of them had temple recommends. At that time, most people were saying that their participation in Mormon feminism was helping them to stay in the church because it was helping them to negotiate and navigate those difficult points and to give them resources and community and support where maybe they would've just left if they hadn't had community and resources and support to stay in the church. And then at other times, Mormon feminists, in the example of people leaving has helped people leave. Mormon feminism both helps people to stay in the church if that is what their goal is and it helps people to

---

[9] See http://www.religjournal.com/articles/article_view.php?id=80

leave if that is what their goal is. And I think that
the community...

GT: 00:37:45   Let me stop you for a second. Was that your goal?

Sara: 00:37:46   To leave? No, but...

GT: 00:37:52   Because the reason I'm asking that is because
there are going to be people who will say, "Well,
if I support it, then I've got one foot out the
door."

Sara: 00:37:58   Right. It's tricky. I'm trying to gather my thoughts
and figure out the right starting point here. The
whole idea of Mormon feminism, helping people
to stay or to leave, I relate to that and I resonate
with that. I think it didn't so much--well from
personal experience I'll say this. My faith crisis or
my big turning point was when I went to the
temple when I was 21. I was about to get married
and I went and received my endowment the week
before my wedding. I had no idea but walking into
the temple I felt completely clear and completely
hundred percent all in with the church. And
leaving the temple I felt like everything had
changed and I didn't know who God was
anymore. And that was very uncomfortable and
what I needed at that point, what I wanted more
than anything was to see examples of people who
had a difficult time with the church for whatever
reason, and still stayed because I wanted to stay
more than anything. But I didn't know, you know,
looking at my family and my ward. It seemed like
everybody was just really comfortable. And so, I
thought, "Well, how do I stay if I'm not

comfortable and if I have questions? Right? And so Mormon feminism, the people I met, the stories I read, really did help me to stay for 10 years. And because of all these external events: excommunication, exclusion policy, Mormon #MeToo, and sexual abuse, and stuff. I think I have also seen examples that convinced me that there was also a way to leave in a healthy way. Not that that was what I wanted to do, but when I felt that spiritual prompting, that that's what my next step was, I felt okay. I have seen from these people's examples that I can do that, and I can still be a spiritual person.

Sara: 00:39:54   I can still have a strong relationship with God. I can still care. I can still be loving. And so, for me, it's not so much about helping you do whatever you want to do, but showing you that there are different options, and giving you the empowerment to say, "Okay, since I know all these options are available to me, which one feels right? Which one do I really want? Do I want to say and have maybe like an uncomfortable activity level or whatever? Do I want to do that? Do I want to leave?" You know, whatever it is, you kind of see that there are possibilities that you can figure out which one you want.

Nancy: 00:40:37   And I would even say too that that question of "Oh well, Mormon feminism makes women leave." Or you know, that assumption really de-centers the idea that there are problems in the LDS Church and there are problems with the way in which the LDS community treats women and LGBT people and people of color and others. And, that's the problem. And the Mormon feminism was to try and help make that easier. And so, the problem isn't with the feminism, the problem is structural in the LDS church and if you don't belong to a group that can be sometimes seen as an outcast or maybe if you are a woman, you're totally happy and the church is working for you, that's great. But, there needs to be more space and that excluding women in particular ways, excluding LGBT people in particular ways, that creates very real difficulties for those people and their families in the church and so their church activity is not a happy life-giving thing. And, and that's what needs addressing. That's what needs addressing. That's where the problems and the structural issues lie.

Sara: 00:41:58   Not in the response.

Nancy: 00:41:58   Right.

GT: 00:42:02   So another question I had was, I wanted you to talk a little bit more about your survey. I want to flesh that out. You said that you did that survey back in, I want to say 2013.

Nancy: 00:42:10   2013.

GT: 00:42:10   And 70 percent were active.

Nancy: 00:42:14   70-ish percent were active. Yeah.

GT: 00:42:17   And so, I believe at Mormon History Association you gave another follow-up to that. Can you talk about what has changed since 2013?

Nancy: <u>00:42:26</u>

Yeah. I did a follow-up survey in 2015 with Jessica Finnegan,[10] my writing and academic research partner. And that activity rate was much lower. This is after John Dehlin's excommunication, but before the Exclusion policy, so early 2015. And those activity rates were not the same. They were much lower, and that's what I expected to find. But I think it's also fair to say that when the church excommunicated people publicly for doing things like asking church leaders to pray about the potential of women's ordination and the church kind of slaps that down and says, "No, you can't ask. You can ask questions, but you can't ask questions." Or, you can't ask that question, or a woman can't ask that question or however you want to frame it. It's like there's a lot of--people lose trust. And, in Mormonism we often conflate trust and faith in God with faith in the LDS Church and trust in the LDS Church as though those are absolutely the same thing and you can't actually peel them apart because they are one in the same. And Mormon feminism helped me to see that they were different things. That the LDS Church was a man-made institution trying to respond to feelings about God's call and place in the world. But that didn't always line up with my own personal experiences of God. And it turns out that lots of women and other people feel the same way and that maybe I also learned that the LDS Church didn't have a monopoly on God. And there were other ways to access God. Sorry, I forgot what the question was.

---

[10] See https://tinyurl.com/yd2pr68a

Sara: 00:44:10   The survey.

GT: 00:44:11   Let me just follow up with that. Because one of
the things you said was there was a pretty steep
decline in activity rates. 70% to 50%, is that what
you said?

Nancy: 00:44:19   Probably something like that. I don't have all the
numbers in in my mind.

GT: 00:44:25   So I think I might have asked you this, but it
wasn't on camera. Do you think that LDS Church
leaders have noticed? Is it causing concern that at
least the females are losing some activity? Or is it
so small that it doesn't really matter? It's a
necessary thing. We had to get rid of these few
people.

Sara: 00:44:49   I can't really speak for them. I don't really know
what happens in the Church Office Building and I
can speculate, but I'm not sure that that speaks to
any of the realities.

GT: 00:44:59   The reason why I asked, I remember in June we
had the 40th anniversary of the revelation on
priesthood[11] that allowed blacks to come to come
to [temple.] I was actually a bit surprised. I want
to say it was in the Deseret News.[12] I was quite
surprised actually that some people had been
upset with the 1978 revelation.

---

[11] See https://www.lds.org/church/news/all-are-equal-prophet-proclaims-at-be-one-celebration?lang=eng

[12] It was the Salt Lake Tribune. See
https://www.sltrib.com/news/polygamy/2018/05/25/right-after-the-mormon-church-gave-blacks-the-priesthood-a-polygamous-offshoot-saw-its-ranks-grow/

Nancy: 00:45:24   Yes.

GT: 00:45:24   While the numbers were small, a lot of these people that were upset by President Kimball's revelation, actually joined some of the fundamentalist groups.

Both: 00:45:36   Yeah, right.

GT: 00:45:36   While in the LDS Church it was a very small number. For the fundamentalists it was a real shot in the arm.

Sara: 00:45:49   It was a big number.

GT: 00:45:49   It really helped grow their numbers.

Both: 00:45:49   Right.

GT: 00:45:49   So I am wondering. Last year when I attended Sunstone, I talked with John Hamer and Lach MacKay the Sunday following Sunstone. In talking there, Lach actually gave the Sunday School lesson.[13] Have you ever heard Lach speak?

Nancy: 00:46:12   Yes.

GT: 00:46:12   He's awesome. That was one of the best Sunday School lessons ever. He was fantastic, and we talked about that in the previous interview. But one of the things that the people in that congregation in Salt Lake City said, and it seems like the November Exclusion Policy…

---

[13] See our interview at https://gospeltangents.com/2018/01/24/surprising-word-wisdom-insights-apostle/

Sara: 00:46:22   The Turning point.

GT: 00:46:23   It might've been Kate Kelly that got the ball rolling, but that was like the final straw for a lot of people. I know that that congregation in Salt Lake City exploded.

Sara: 00:46:32   That's interesting.

GT: 00:46:32   They went from just a few, maybe a dozen or two to over 100 LDS people LDS people that joined the Community of Christ, kind of like you did.

Sara: 00:46:46   Right.

GT: 00:46:47   And so I'm wondering, do the numbers have to be bigger before the LDS Church says, "Maybe we made a mistake?" Or is it, is it more like with the polygamists, it's just a small number. For the Community of Christ, it's great. Or to the fundamentals In 1978 it was great because it expanded the numbers. But overall, it's just a small number. So, it's not worth it to change.

Nancy: 00:47:10   I think that--Sorry, do you [want to answer?]

Sara: 00:47:13   I mean my guess, completely uninformed guess as somebody who doesn't work for the church or anything, my guess is that there's not a lot of consideration of the possibility that they've made a mistake on any front. And, I think the men who run the Church and the bureaucracy that supports them by and large really believes in their prophetic calling and the fact that God wouldn't let them do something wrong, wouldn't let them lead the church astray. So, I could see people being disappointed or disheartened or whatever to see people leave. But there's always the explanation of having it being the last days and needing to sort of get rid of the X. I forget the...

Nancy: 00:48:13   Right. We're just kind of sinful apostates.

Sara: 00:48:14   Right. And, we need to kind of clear the field, make sure that only the most dedicated, are there. And so, I would be very surprised if there was a concern over the number of people who've left following these particular things.

GT: 00:48:32   You don't think LDS leaders are concerned about it? It's a small number.

Sara: 00:48:35   I mean individually they may, right. I would say it depends on what you mean by concerned. They might have a feeling of disappointment or regret might be too big of a word, but a feeling of "Oh, I wish that weren't the case." But concern that's actionable? I don't see it personally. But then again, I'm not in a position where I necessarily would see it.

Nancy: 00:48:57   I've heard rumors about such things and such concerns, particularly in southern Utah about Community of Christ and the Snuffer movement, taking people away from LDS Church. I think that the actual realistic numbers are very small. But I don't know if church leaders understand why people would change traditions very well. I think that that is a really interesting research question.

GT: 00:49:32   Well let me throw out another thing. So, I interviewed Michael Quinn[14] on Gospel Tangents. It will be out here in a couple of days and one of the things that he said that really surprised me, he'd written a chapter in Maxine Hanks' book[15]. Are you related to Maxine, by the way?

Sara: 00:49:55   I am related to Maxine.

GT: 00:49:57   Oh you are? I did now know that.

Sara: 00:49:57   Maxine Hanks, I only met her a few years ago. But yeah, we're distant cousins, the way Mormons are with polygamy. Yeah.

GT: 00:50:07   Oh wow, that's cool. So anyway, we talked about the Manifesto in 1890 about polygamy and there really was pretty much almost a schism there. So that's where the fundamentalist church started. With my interview with Matt Harris, one of the big concerns with President Kimball was to have another schism over blacks and the priesthood. And so, I asked Michael about Ordain Women. First of all, one of the things he said that I thought was very interesting was women already have the priesthood. They don't need priesthood. They only need priesthood office.

Sara: 00:50:42   That's what he argues Maxine's book.

---

[14] See our interview at https://gospeltangents.com/2018/08/23/women-have-priesthood-since-1843/
[15] The book is called "Women and Authority: Re-emerging Mormon Feminism." It is found at https://amzn.to/2CUfGR9

GT: 00:50:44 And so, but he also said, if we were to ordain women, he fears, just like with the Community of Christ in 1984, they really had a split over that issue, really a schism. He's concerned that the LDS Church would have a similar schism. And I was surprised because we went through 1978. I wouldn't call that a schism. There were some people. How do you feel about that?

Sara: 00:51:10 I think there are a lot more women in the church than there were black people in the church in 1978 and every member of the church, every man in the church knows a woman and probably lives with a woman. And not everybody in 1978 knew a black person or had a close relationship. And so, I think the impact that it has on people's lives would be very different than that revelation was for the average white member of the Church in 1978. If they announced the ordination of women tomorrow, that would change everybody's family system in a really big way and I think it was difficult for people to accept in 1978 and even those who did accept it, it was even harder to change their mindset to actually deal with all the built up prejudices that they had received from the church. I mean that's still an ongoing process. And so, I think it would be exaggerated in that hypothetical situation because the impact would be larger.

Must Women Be Ordained?

Introduction

Early Mormon women blessed by laying on of hands. If the practice returned, would that be good enough for the Ordain Women movement, or do they require ordination? Nancy Ross and Sara Hanks answer that question. Check out our conversation....

Nancy: 00:52:16 So, a couple of years ago I was part of a group of scholars who did a couple of big surveys. One was of 50,000 Mormons. So, we asked the question, if the prophet was to announce tomorrow or the next General Conference that there were going to ordain women, would you accept that? And 90 percent said yes. They would accept that. Even if the numbers for people who are expressing a desire for the ordination of women were different. And I think when you look at the Community of Christ case, and I've heard a lot of people talk about this in the short time that I've been in Community of Christ, which is that the upper leadership had done their own prep work for preparing themselves for the ordination of women so that they can make it okay for them, but they hadn't done a lot of prep work and advanced work for preparing the whole church for that.

Nancy: 00:53:10 And that, when a similarly big change came in 2013 when the World Church Organization decided that they would allow for full inclusion of LGBT people. They did a lot of advanced work. And they created ways for congregations to disagree. So, a congregation can be in faithful disagreement over the issue of full inclusion of LGBT people. And they did a lot of advanced work in a lot of different places so that when the vote happened, yes, not everybody was happy about it. And, they did vote for the full inclusion, but there was an acceptance that they could all be one church and I'm sure that there were people who left, but it wasn't the numbers of people who left in the 1980s because they did all this advanced work.

Nancy: 00:54:06   And my guess is that should another prospect of another really big, social change kind of happen in the church that again, they would do a lot of advanced legwork. How can we get buy in? How can we get people on board? How can we educate? How can we show that this is different? And I've talked to Lach MacKay about this and he's like, "You know, if we could go back to 1984, we would be talking about this differently and we would be doing different kinds of outreach work so that there wouldn't be that same kind of schism at the end." And, so I think that they have learned from their own process of change, how to create smoother change and how to facilitate change, not only at a decision-making level or with the decision-making body but with the whole church and I think that that's been an important lesson for them. The change for the full inclusion of women was a huge change, but now they know how to make change better and deeper and in ways that the result of that will be more inclusive. And, I think that's important lessons to learn.

GT: 00:55:10   Are you still a member of Ordain Women?

Nancy: 00:55:13   I mean, I still have a profile of a website, and I'm still supportive of the organization.

GT: 00:55:16   And you're being ordained this Sunday anyway.

Nancy: 00:55:16   That's right.

Sara: 00:55:20   Ordained woman.

Nancy: 00:55:21   Yes, Ordain Women! We're doing it.

GT: 00:55:22   You're going to be ordained. My question is actually two questions. Number one, what if in say October General Conference, President Nelson got up and said, "Okay, we're going to go back to the idea that women can lay hands on the sick like they used to do even into the early 20th century. Would that be good enough for Ordain Women? Or, do you think that women still need to be ordained to priesthood office?

Nancy: 00:56:04   Do you want to comment?

Sara: 00:56:05   I would say nothing less than full inclusion and full opportunity for every member of the church would be quote unquote sufficient. Any step in the direction of progress on any subject, in any community is great. Any step. Great.

GT: 00:56:24   So you would welcome the laying on of hands.

Sara: 00:56:25   Oh, I would welcome that completely. I would be so excited about that. I mean I would be overjoyed. But in terms of Ordain Women as an organization, I think they chose their name very specifically. It's Ordain Women, not like give women--I mean, it would be a very long name, but it's not like Give Women More Opportunities. It's Ordain Women.

Sara: 00:56:45   I remember shortly after Ordain Women was launched, Kate Kelly did a radio interview somewhere in the Salt Lake area and a caller asked, "So what? You won't be satisfied until women can be the prophet?" And she was like "Yeah, nothing less than full inclusion at every level is going to be enough." So, I would say, until women and men and black people and brown people and white people and LGBTQ people, until everybody has the same opportunities before them for inclusion in the church and for opportunities to access power and minister and all those things, until that's what we see, there is still room to grow.

Nancy: 00:57:34   I agree with all of that. Absolutely. Because the goal here with the ordination of women is to make the church, the way I see it is to make the church a safer, better place for women. And it would be awesome if there was an acknowledgement that women could give blessings in the open. That would be great, but that doesn't make the church fully a safer place for women. That doesn't put more women on decision making councils where women's needs and a diversity of women's needs are acknowledged and accounted for in a decision-making process. Then the LDS Church, ordination and priesthood power are paramount. So, women don't really achieve full equality unless they have access to that same power.

GT: 00:58:20 There is no separate by equal.

Sara: 00:58:22 There's really not, there's not.

GT: 00:58:26 Alright, but you would welcome if women could start doing blessings of the sick or whatever.

Nancy: 00:58:31 Yes. I mean we know a lot of women who do that.

Sara: 00:58:34 Yeah, we do and it would be amazing if it could be. I mean I would on a personal note, like I think of my aunts and my grandmas and my mom and the women that I know who are so faithfully LDS, they would never think of doing something that the church wasn't okay with. If they could have that opportunity and to do it in a way that was in a church meeting like that. I mean--tears. Like it would be incredible.

GT: 00:59:00 Well, let me ask you this because I've got a couple of sisters and we've talked about this, and they are like, "I don't want the priesthood."

Sara: 00:59:08 Sure.

GT: 00:59:08 "I don't want any part of that." I've got one sister says "I've got enough to do. I don't want any more responsibility."

Both: 00:59:17 Sure.

GT: 00:59:17 How would you respond to that?

Sara: 00:59:20   I think it would depend on the situation, but I think on one front, on one hand I'd be like, "Okay, great." Like I understand that you don't need to have something that you don't want, but it also doesn't square. That sort of response that I hear so often from women in the church, it's very much at odds with the way that they talk about what priesthood is for their husbands or their sons or their brothers. They talk about the priesthood as something that assists them in the work that they have to do. They talk about priesthood as a way to exercise God's power and to bless the people that they love. You know, I go back to the early days of my marriage with my husband and health problems that we had and wanting a child that we couldn't have yet.

Sara: 01:00:04   My husband was able to give me blessings of comfort and to speak to me with a voice that was his, but also had God in it and I couldn't do the same for him. He was hurting too. He had to go to a home teacher or the bishop or his dad. And those are important relationships, but I wanted to be able to do that for him. And I would want to be able to do that for my kids too, to give them comfort or to show them, to tell them what I think God would want them to hear. And so, when women say, "Oh, I don't want it. Oh, I already have enough to do. Oh, the extra responsibility," I wonder if you take the average Mormon woman who gives that response, would she want her son to feel that way about the priesthood? Would she want her son coming up at the age of 12 to say, "Oh no thanks. I have enough responsibility. I don't want that responsibility." Or would she want them to welcome the opportunity to exercise the priesthood? She would probably want her son to welcome that. Why would she want any different for herself or for her daughter? That's the contradiction that I see. If a woman doesn't want the priesthood or a man doesn't want the priesthood, don't have it. Like I think that's perfectly valid.

GT: 01:01:27   That's interesting because I know in the early days of the LDS Church, I've talked with a few historians and they said that it was pretty typical for a man, when he was baptized, he was immediately ordained.[16] That's pretty much-- we've followed that for going on 200 years. But it doesn't sound like that happened in the Community of Christ. Not everybody is just ordained. Is that correct?

Nancy: 01:01:50   Not everybody is ordained. No. Ordination is something that has a particular calling. So, leaders, usually local leaders, people who know people well will sense that maybe somebody has a call and so there is no blanket ordination of everyone. Yeah, so ordination isn't automatically given out and children are never ordained.

Sara: 01:02:14   Right.

GT: 01:02:14   Yeah. So how old do you have to be?

---

[16] See out interview with Dr. Mark Staker: https://gospeltangents.com/2017/03/03/black-pete-former-slave-becomes-first-black-mormon/

Nancy: <u>01:02:16</u>   You have to be an adult.

GT: <u>01:02:17</u>   You need to be an adult. So, 18?

Nancy: <u>01:02:18</u>   Yes, that's my understanding. Yes.

GT: <u>01:02:21</u>   So you weren't immediately ordained upon baptism.

Nancy: <u>01:02:24</u>   No.

GT: <u>01:02:24</u>   It's taken a year and a half.

Nancy: <u>01:02:27</u>   Yeah, it's taken a year, and it doesn't happen for everyone, but it's also not something that... So yes, I will be ordained on Sunday and that's something that's happening and I'm very excited about it, but I do all kinds of things in and for my congregation short of blessing and passing communion, everything else. Everything else is available to me except for the sacramental stuff. And so, it's not like, "Oh I can't make decisions or help facilitate decision making within my congregation."

Sara: <u>01:03:01</u>   Not until you have the priesthood.

Nancy: <u>01:03:02</u>   It's like I've been doing all these things which is so much more than I was able to do as an LDS woman. You know, I have the key to the building, the glorious key of the building and I help facilitate decision making and I organize stuff and no one's like "You don't have the authority to do that." Because that's just what I've been doing, and I have enjoyed that sense of just ministering, without priesthood. And soon I will have that, and that will be an additional thing that I have. And so, then I will be able to kind of bless and pass communion and do some other things as well, but I've been able to do a lot and much more than I was able to do previously as you know, a Relief Society sister and that makes me feel happy and valued, included without ordination.

GT: 01:03:47   It sounds like you don't miss Relief Society either.

Sara: 01:03:51   I think Relief Society can be really awesome and I think I've had moments in my life when Relief Society was really awesome and wonderful and good. But it's not that way for everyone and it isn't necessarily that way consistently for people.

GT: 01:04:07   So this is another question I have because I have to say I don't think I'm the target demographic for Feminist Mormon Housewives, is that right?

Sara: 01:04:14   You might be.

GT: 01:04:16   I mean there are a few men.

Sara: 01:04:21   Oh yes, there are men in the book.

GT: 01:04:21   I know Ziff. There's a few of them, a few men in there. I tried to read those. But, I do want to ask you your favorite essays in just a minute here. But, Lisa created Feminist Mormon Housewives as a place, I think more for women than for men. Not that men can't come.

Sara: 01:04:36   Right. That's exactly right.

Nancy: 01:04:40   Yeah.

Sara: 01:04:40   It's for women, but men are welcome.

GT: 01:04:40   Yeah. But I don't. And I've read Feminist Mormon Housewives, if somebody points at a post, I'll read it, but I'm not the target audience really.

Sara: 01:04:51   That's true.

GT: 01:04:51   So it does seem like with Relief Society, it's a place for women. With Feminist Mormon Housewives, it's a place for women. That's who it is. So is there a place for Relief Society and ordination in the LDS Church.

Nancy: 01:05:06   Oh yeah. I mean that's how Relief Society was set up.

GT: 01:05:09   Well how come the Community of Christ got rid of Relief Society?

Nancy: 01:05:12   Because it saw Relief Society as I think a narrower group, and in many ways to kind of support polygamy. And so, they don't do that. But I don't they're less effective because they don't do that.

Sara: 01:05:26   Right. There are different ways to set up churches that can all be effective, and all have their gifts. And Community of Christ decided that that didn't fit with their goals exactly. But it's not hard for me to imagine a setting where a church would have a group like Relief Society that was very specifically about women. And also have opportunities for people of any gender to be ordained.

Nancy: 01:05:54 Right. And it's also important to point out that the whole history of the Relief Society wasn't inclusive of all or most women and that it was only, I think in the 1970s when all women were seen as automatically part of Relief Society. So, the Relief Society has its own history and I think that there is some complicated pieces of that too.

Sara: 01:06:11 Yeah, definitely.

Nancy: 01:06:12 So yeah.

GT: 01:06:14 So, you could see, I'll direct this to you Sara, you could see the LDS Church ordaining women and maintaining Relief Society, not as separate quorum or would the elders meet together?

Sara: 01:06:25 I mean, I don't know how. I think there are any number of ways that it could be organized, but I have room in my imagination for a church that still had a third hour class for women and a third hour class for men and a third hour class for young kids, and also made room for ordination.

GT: 01:06:45 Would the elders, these male elders meet together, and the female elders meet together?

Sara: 01:06:49 Maybe.

Nancy: 01:06:50 But Sara, I can envision a church that's only two hours and women's ordination. I'll one-up you on my vision.

Sara: 01:06:58 Can you imagine? Yeah, I think there's value to be had in gender specific spaces, and so maybe they would rename the class, so it wasn't the elders and the other elders.

GT: 01:07:09   The male elders and the sister elders.

Sara: 01:07:09   I don't know what they would do or how they would do it. I mean I think that there would, even if ordination was offered to everybody on equal playing field, there would still be value in women meeting together and in men meeting together and then you know, elderly people, people of whatever groups meeting together, to kind of share and relate with people who understand a lot of what your experience has been.

Nancy: 01:07:33   Absolutely. And I would also say that the way in which the LDS Church divides groups of people into men and women also leaves out a lot of other people

Sara: 01:07:44   It does.

Nancy: 01:07:44   And, it can create difficulties for trans people, for gender non binary people.

Sara: 01:07:50   It definitely does.

Nancy: 01:07:50   And that not focusing so much on the kind of male/female binary also leaves space for additional inclusion to be like all adults have the potential to be ordained and everybody has these different gifts and they can all contribute to our church communities and help build the kingdom of God.

Sara: 01:08:10   Yeah. And, and what if there were options for people to go to different classes or whatever based on their interests and not so much on like whatever category they fit into. There's lots of ways it could be.

Feminist Favorites: Where Must We Stand?

Introduction

In our final conversation with Sara Hanks and Dr. Nancy Ross, I'll ask them what their favorite essays were. Check out our conversation...

GT: 01:08:29   So what I would like to do is we've talked a lot about Kate Kelly and that. Let's go back to the book. I just want to point out a few of my favorites. I'd like to ask you guys, what are some of your favorites?

GT: 01:08:40   Joanna Brooks.[17] I love Joanna. She is awesome. Claudia Reppen,[18] the Faithful Dissident.[19] We've been buddies for a while. So, I really enjoy Claudia. I guess the one real surprise to me, because I kind of know Joanna, and Claudia from other things. Kalani Tonga.[20] She's a fantastic writer.

Sara: 01:09:05   She's amazing. She was the person making the funny faces earlier.

GT: 01:09:06   Oh, Okay. So yeah. So, can you guys, and I don't know if you should have favorites since it's your book.

---

[17] See Joanna's posts at
http://www.feministmormonhousewives.org/?s=joanna+brooks
[18] See Claudia's posts at
http://www.feministmormonhousewives.org/?s=faithful+dissident
[19] See Claudia's blog at http://thefaithfuldissident.blogspot.com/
[20] See Kalani's posts at http://www.feministmormonhousewives.org/?s=kalani

Nancy: <u>01:09:11</u>   Oh we do.

Sara: <u>01:09:12</u>   We're allowed to have favorites.

GT: <u>01:09:14</u>   So tell us your favorites.

Sara: <u>01:09:16</u>   I think one that comes to mind for me is one that was written by a woman named Trina Thomas Nelson. It's called, "Claim yourself. Finding validation and purpose without institutional approval."[21] And it starts with a personal story of hers because she's a black woman. Her parents were members of the church, black members of the church prior to the 1978, official declaration,[22] and she talks about seeing her parents claim a space in a church that didn't really have room for them to fully be. And how they claimed their right to be there without the institution's approval. And she said sometimes that's what you have to do. Like you can want the institution to approve of you. You can want the institution to accommodate you or meet you where you are and sometimes it just won't. And then the choice becomes yours. Like, do I believe enough in my own belonging to just claim a space anyway? And so, I love that one. There's an essay in here that Lisa wrote about the Parable of the Ten Virgins[23] that I really love.

GT: <u>01:10:29</u>   Lisa is a great writer.

---

[21] See http://www.feministmormonhousewives.org/2014/05/claim-yourself-finding-validation-and-purpose-without-institutional-approval/
[22] See https://www.lds.org/scriptures/dc-testament/od/2
[23] See https://www.feministmormonhousewives.org/2012/07/the-parable-of-the-ten-virgins/

Sara: 01:10:30   She is a great writer, and Lisa is, I mean, as you would imagine as the founder of the blog, the one who was writing the entire time. She has the most pieces in the book. There are multiple posts from Emily Summerhayes that I really love. I mean, I do have favorites, but I probably have like a dozen of them, so I'll stop there. And I'll also mention at the end of the book, there are extra essays that weren't ever published on the blog and in fact were never published anywhere else that are just from members of the community reflecting on this time. There's one from Claudia. There's one from Kalani. There's one from Lori Winder Stromberg, Misha McGriggs and a few others. And I love those too. Even though it took longer to make this book than I expected to. I love that we can kind of look back on it with a little bit of distance and reflect on this time and all that it taught us.

GT: 01:11:24   How about you Nancy?

Nancy: 01:11:25   I have a bunch of different favorite posts. I think when I was I was reading the blog, as they were kind of coming out, my most favorite posts was by Fran, and the post is called "A [Short] History of my Breasts,"[24] where she kind of talks about modesty and the way in which people have responded to and interacted with her body and the difficulty of that experience over her lifetime and coming to kind of accept her body for what it was. And I just loved that post. And that's in the

---

[24] See https://www.feministmormonhousewives.org/2013/08/a-short-history-of-my-breasts/

book. I really like and resonate with Lisa's post early in the book called, "I'm a Slug,"[25] about the kind of periodic emotional breakdown that she has for over being a stay at home mom and just how it's so overwhelming and emotionally intense. And, there's a problem with that, right? Like it's a problem that we kind of break down like almost on a schedule.

GT: 01:12:16   I feel like we have done a disservice, because there are a lot of posts about motherhood and we didn't really talk about that.

Sara: 01:12:23   That's ok. It's alright.

GT: 01:12:25   They are the Feminist Mormon Housewives after all. And we really did neglect that quite a bit, but it's been kind of interesting.

Nancy: 01:12:30   Yeah. That was just a really kind of key post for me and even going back today, I'm so glad that when I was a young mom and really struggling that I was able to encounter a post like that because that just gave me a lot of comfort. You know, these are very personal responses to these posts.

GT: 01:12:45   And that's one of the things, since you mentioned that. One of the things that I have found, I'm more of a history nerd. I love history, whether it's modern or distant history, but the one thing about pretty much almost every essay I read was, they were so personal. Like you could see inside

---

[25] See https://www.feministmormonhousewives.org/2006/09/slug/

the person's soul and so it was very touching in that respect. It wasn't this dry esoteric history stuff that I like.

Sara: 01:13:14   No, it's not. It's not historically based, it's not academic. It's mostly people just writing from their own experience and even if they do have commentary on a larger issue like polygamy or like the church's position on Prop eight, a lot of it is very grounded in personal experience. I think that's the way we're brought up as Mormon women and probably as women in general. To relate to our world is from that very personal place and how we connect with other people. So yeah, I think it made the whole blog very approachable because you didn't feel like you had any sort of barrier to entry, like you had to have read certain books before you could participate.

GT: 01:13:53   Right. And you can pick that book and you could open it up to any page. It's not something that you have to read sequentially.

Both: 01:13:58   No, it's not.

GT: 01:14:01   You can do that, and it is interesting to see the themes, especially over the years as the themes change. But you could literally open up anywhere. In fact, I remember, because I a Kindle version on my thing. I couldn't remember where I was, and it I didn't keep my place and I'm like, "Well, I'll just start at the end." I started at the end, I went back to the beginning. I went in the middle, and so I've been all over the place, not sequentially at all and it was perfectly fine.

Nancy: 01:14:29   Yes.

GT: 01:14:29   So. So that was one of the neat things about that book.

Nancy: 01:14:32   Yeah. And in many ways, the kind of raw expose' of emotion and complication of the way we feel about the lives we live is one of the most beautiful things about the book. To acknowledge all the difficulty and complexity, you know, if we want to be like, "Oh, well Mormon women are like this and their lives are like this." And I think that what the book and the essays in the book of Mormon women are all like this [she waves her hands wildly.]

Nancy: 01:14:57   And their feelings are about that are all like this. But, I love the way, and I've always loved the blog for the way in which it spoke to the real messiness of real Mormon women's lives. Yeah.

Sara: 01:15:08   Yeah.

GT: 01:15:08   It was definitely very real. So, the last question I want to ask you, why did you pick the title "Where We Must Stand?" Where must we must we stand?

Sara: 01:15:18   Aha! Where must we stand? Well, the very short answer to that is that we chose it from a blog post. It was a blog post that was written in 2010 by Lisa. It was very shortly after (listeners might remember this) President Boyd K. Packer gave a talk in General Conference where he kind of rubbed some people the wrong way when it came to LGBTQ issues saying, "Why would God do that to anyone?" It was just a tough moment and the responses that were happening on the blog, both in posts in comments were very heated. People [were] being very upset with him and upset with the institution of the church. People then feeling like they had to defend the church and it was just a tough moment. And Lisa wrote this post called "Faithful and Feminist Toward Balance."[26] And she talked about how this wasn't a blog where we could be 100 percent all about defending the church and the church is 100 percent right all the time. It couldn't be a 100 percent faith promoting blog. It also couldn't be a 100 percent faith denying blog because we were Mormons. You know? We had faith. We had testimonies. We had some attraction to parts of the Gospel.

Sara: 01:16:32   And she said right in the middle of that divide is where we must stand, where you can go to Sunday School for the faith promoting stuff. You can go to a secular feminist blog for the totally unreligious stuff, but we're not either of those things and we have to stand in the middle and it's not comfortable, but we have to stand here. So, it was the place that we had to stand in or that FMH really tried to stand in was finding a balance between feminism and faith, making sure that neither one was neglected, neither one was held up as more important, but kind of integrating both of those and seeing how we could do it.

Nancy: 01:17:14   Yeah.

---

[26] See https://www.feministmormonhousewives.org/2010/10/3319/

GT: 01:17:15   Well, it's been great having you both on *Gospel Tangents*.

Sara: 01:17:17   Thank you.

GT: 01:17:19   Do you have any last thoughts you'd like to share with us?

Nancy: 01:17:21   Read the book.

Sara: 01:17:23   Yeah, read it. Read the book. Buy the book. You can get on Amazon[27] if you want. A dollar from every book sold goes to a scholarship fund that you can actually read about in the book. It's called the Tracy Mckay Scholarship Fund. It's for single moms pursuing their education and the first recipient of it, in 2013, I believe was a woman named Tracy McKay who was a member of the community and she writes about her experience with that. And it's been awarded every year since to a single mom going to school. So yeah, we would love it if you read the book and underlined it up and loved it and shared it with people and reviewed it on Amazon. I mean, we're just, we're really proud of the book and we're so happy.

GT: 01:18:02   A good review, right?

Sara: 01:18:02   I mean, yeah, five stars please. Anything less will not do. We're really happy that it exists. And, we just love the community, the very messy weird community that it came from. And, I'm excited to see what the future holds. I mean, this is one little aside, but what's interesting to me is that there's

---

[27] Can be purchased at https://amzn.to/2q9knOM

such a long history of Mormon Feminism back to the beginning days of the church. Definitely in the 70's and 80's and 90's. Lisa Butterworth started this blog in 2004 and she didn't know about any of that. She wasn't carrying on a tradition, she just was a Mormon woman who was a feminist and I think sometimes us old timers can kind of fret about what's going to happen next and where is this going to go? And I think you never know where a flower's going to bloom and start something. We don't know what's going to happen next. But I'm excited to see. That's it.

GT: 01:19:00   Any last thoughts Nancy?

Sara: 01:19:00   No, I think Sara sums it up pretty well.

GT: 01:19:06   One thing that I do want to just point out here, one of the things that I liked. I believe, and correct me if I'm wrong, at the beginning of every chapter, you wrote a little history. Was it you who did that?

Sara: 01:19:16   Yes, yes.

Nancy: 01:19:18   Sara started that and I kind of edited some of those and added so it was a collaborative process. Yeah.

GT: 01:19:24   I thought that was great, because you would talk about the new blogs that started. I noticed that Wheat and Tares[28] was not mentioned.

Nancy: 01:19:30   Because *Wheat and Tares* is older.

---

[28] See https://wheatandtares.org/

Sara:	<u>01:19:31</u>	It's pre-FMH.
GT:	<u>01:19:35</u>	No, 2009.
Sara:	<u>01:19:35</u>	Not *Wheat and Tares, Times and Seasons*. All these blogs with their something and something names, *Wheat and Tares, Doves and Serpents*...
Nancy:	<u>01:19:42</u>	There should be a Mormon blog called "Something and Something."
GT:	<u>01:19:46</u>	I blog at *Wheat and Tares*.
Sara:	<u>01:19:46</u>	My bad!
Nancy:	<u>01:19:48</u>	I apologize that we left you out. I'm sorry.
Sara:	<u>01:19:50</u>	Our apologies. Sorry.
GT:	<u>01:19:55</u>	Thanks again! It was wonderful meeting you two.
Sara:	<u>01:19:54</u>	Thank you.
Nancy:	<u>01:19:55</u>	Good to meet you.
GT:	<u>01:19:59</u>	Thanks again for being on *Gospel Tangents*.
Both:	<u>01:19:59</u>	Sure. Thank you. Thank you.

Epilogue

<table>
<tr><td>GT:</td><td>01:20:01</td><td>I hope you enjoyed our conversation with Sara Hanks and Dr. Nancy Ross of Dixie State University. I'd like to thank them both for spending so much time talking with us and sharing their experiences and learning more about Mormon Feminism. If you'd like a transcript of this, please click the Yellow Subscribe Button at https://GospelTangents.com and I'll send you this and all future transcripts. Also, if you'd like a paperback like we've got here, those are available at our website at Amazon.com. Just do a search for Gospel Tangents. Please get all updates at our Facebook page at https://Facebook.com/GospelTangents. We're also on twitter @GospelTangents. You can also get transcripts individually at our website, GospelTangents.com/shop. Finally, make sure that you subscribe on Apple podcast page. Just do a quick search for a Gospel Tangents there and give us a five-star review while you're at it. Thanks again for listening. Your support helps create more Mormon history classes and podcasts such as this, and so I really appreciate you listening. Please share with your friends.</td></tr>
</table>

Check out our other videos that we've done on Youtube! We hope you'll use this as a valuable resource to learn more about Mormon history!

Additional Resources:

To learn more about women's studies, check out some of our other interviews!

Jonathan Stapley – The Power of Godliness

Dr. Jonathan Stapley Discusses evolution of LDS Priesthood Ordinances

165: Elder Oaks Groundbreaking Talk on Women & Priesthood (Stapley)
https://gospeltangents.com/2018/06/15/elder-oaks-groundbreaking-address-women-priesthood/

164: The Mormon Priestess & Ordain Women (Stapley)
https://gospeltangents.com/2018/06/13/the-mormon-priestess-and-ordain-women-part-3/

163: Women Healers in LDS Temples (Stapley)
https://gospeltangents.com/2018/06/10/women-healers-in-lds-temples/

Michael Quinn – Women & Priesthood

Historian Dr. Michael Quinn, author or *Wealth & Corporate Power*

189: <u>Women Have Had Priesthood since 1843!</u> (Quinn)
https://gospeltangents.com/2018/08/23/women-have-priesthood-since-1843/

Newell Bringhurst – Author of Saints, Slaves, and Blacks

Dr. Newell Bringhurst, author of several books on Mormon History

132: <u>Bringhurst's Approach to Controversy</u> (Bringhurst)
https://gospeltangents.com/2018/03/04/bringhursts-approach-controversy/

134: <u>Role of Women in 4 American Religions</u> (Bringhurst)
https://gospeltangents.com/2018/03/10/role-of-women-in-4-american-religions/

Anne Wilde on Modern Polygamy

Anne Wilde, founder of Principle Voices, modern-day Polygamy expert

099: Polygamy & 2002 Olympics (Wilde)
https://gospeltangents.com/2017/11/21/polygamy-2002-olympics/

098: Law of Sarah/Concubines (Wilde)
https://gospeltangents.com/2017/11/22/anne-justify-concubines-law-sarah/

097: Was Jesus a Polygamist? (Wilde)
https://gospeltangents.com/2017/11/20/annes-marriage-jesus-polygamist/

096: Ervil Lebaron: Polygamist, Assassin (Wilde)
https://gospeltangents.com/2017/11/16/ervil-lebaron-polygamist-assassin/

095: FLDS-Centennial Park Rivalry (Wilde)
https://gospeltangents.com/2017/11/14/flds-centennial-park-rivalry/

092: How to Polygamists Feel about Gay Marriage? (Wilde)
https://gospeltangents.com/2017/11/04/how-do-polygamists-feel-about-gay-marriage/

091: 3rd Manifesto Causes Schism: Apostolic United Brethren (Wilde)
https://gospeltangents.com/2017/10/31/third-manifesto-causes-schism-apostolic-united-brethren/

090: Did Woodruff Marry After the 1890 Manifesto? (Wilde)
https://gospeltangents.com/2017/10/29/woodruff-marry-1890-manifesto/

Interview with Remnant LDS Church

Jim Vun Cannon, Counselor in the First Presidency of the Remnant Church of Jesus Christ of Latter Day Saints

We'd also love to have you visit our Amazon Store on our website to see other books on Mormon History. Be sure to check out our blog as well at https://GospelTangents.com to find information about future guests and projects we are working on. We would also like to partner with artists and musicians to produce a documentary on this and other topics. Please email us at GospelTangents@gmail.com if you're interested.

Thank you for your generous support!

9 781729 393987